Original title:

The Anthurium's Anthem

Copyright © 2025 Creative Arts Management OÜ
All rights reserved.

Author: Nolan Kingsley
ISBN HARDBACK: 978-1-80581-911-0
ISBN PAPERBACK: 978-1-80581-438-2
ISBN EBOOK: 978-1-80581-911-0

Muse of the Maroon Petals

In the garden where clowns don leafy hats,
Maroon petals dance with jovial chats.
Bumblebees giggle as they sip on air,
While butterflies wear their best debonair.

A squirrel throws shade from a branch up high,
As the flowers gossip, oh my, oh my!
With whispers of secrets, they jest and tease,
Making the sun drop down on its knees.

Oh, the petals swirl, like a joyous jest,
Each bloom out here trying to look its best.
They wink and they wiggle, such a sight to see,
Pulling pranks on the ants with glee and esprit.

Amidst this hilarity, the day's gallivant,
The bees applaud loudly, "What a splendid plant!"
Nature's own comedy, in colors so bright,
Maroon petals share laughter, a true delight!

Harmony in Hues

In a garden of rainbow cheer,
A flower winks, 'Come here!'
With petals bright and bold,
It struts like it owns the world.

A bee buzzes in for a chat,
'Why so flashy?' asks the gnat.
The flower grins, a cheeky tease,
'I'm just here to steal the breeze!'

Nature's Bold Palette

Dancing under the sun so grand,
A bloom prances on the land.
Colors clash in joyful array,
A party where all come to play.

The butterfly joins in the fun,
With moves that are second to none.
'Look at me!' it flits with grace,
While petals laugh at the race.

The Soul of a Flower

A flower dreams of gone-before,
Of blossoms past and tales galore.
It giggles with the breeze so light,
'Who knew blooms could be such a sight?'

Rooted deep but oh so spry,
A leaf whispers, 'I can fly!'
The flower nods, 'Take a chance,
Don't just stand there—join the dance!'

Whispered Promises of Spring

Springtime giggles, 'Here I am!'
With flowers bright, a lively jam!
Each petal hums a funny tune,
While bees gather 'neath the moon.

The sun shines bright, a daily jest,
While the tulip claims it's the best.
'You can't outshine my radiant hue!'
But hey, who's judging? Me or you?

Melodies of the Garden

In a garden so bright, flowers dance,
With petals that twirl, they take a chance.
Bees buzz like drummers, keeping the beat,
While plants do the cha-cha on leafy feet.

The sun plays the trumpet, rays all around,
Worms wiggle to rhythms beneath the ground.
A tulip sings loud, its voice like a bell,
In this wild orchestration, all's well, all's well!

Nature's Passionate Cry

In the forest, a parrot squawks a tune,
While squirrels are twirling 'neath the bright moon.
The trees sway and giggle with each gentle breeze,
Claiming their fame like they're TV peas!

Caterpillars gossip, they whisper and chat,
While crickets make jokes with laughter so fat.
Nature's a party, come join the fun,
Where every creature shines bright like the sun!

Impressions in Green

Dandelions giggle with their fluffy heads,
Drawing in breezes and dodging their beds.
A ladybug winks, wearing spots like a star,
Sipping on dew in a slipstream bazaar.

Frogs leap like dancers in a wild ballet,
Splashing in puddles, they steal the day.
Trees wear their leaves like a fancy new dress,
In this green gallery, it's anyone's guess!

Aesthetic Roots

Roots underground whisper sweet nothings loud,
Plotting a party, all nature's so proud.
They twist and they turn in a subterranean rave,
Where earthworms do limbo, oh how they behave!

Mushrooms are hats for the critters that roam,
Inviting the sun to their cozy dome.
With laughter and chatter, the soil does sing,
In this earthy fortress, let joy take wing!

Resplendent Resonance

In a garden so bright, oh what a sight,
Petals dance with joy, in morning light.
Leaves whisper secrets, quite the charade,
Bees join the party, buzzing parade.

Colors like laughter, they tickle the air,
Plants in a riot, without a care.
Ivy's got jokes, in a vine-y twist,
Stems sway along, you can't resist.

A flower's delight, in playful jest,
Leaves curtsy low, feeling blessed.
Roots giggle beneath, in silent cheer,
Nature's own comedy, oh so dear.

In this floral circus, all join the fun,
Chasing the shadows, under the sun.
Life's a bouquet, each bloom has a tale,
In this garden of giggles, we shall prevail!

Garden of Emotions

In rows so bright, a lineup of glee,
Sunflowers grinning, as happy as can be.
Tulips tell jokes, with a colorful snort,
In this lively plot, there's never a drought.

Petunias prance, in flamboyant attire,
Daisies throw shade, they never tire.
Pansies sing loud, no voices they lack,
While roses just blush and hold nothing back.

The soil's alive, with a whimsical thrill,
Worms cracking wise, as they wiggle and chill.
A garden of chuckles, where laughter grows wide,
In petals we trust, where joy cannot hide.

So come take a stroll, let your spirits rise,
Gazing at blooms, under sunny skies.
In nature's own laughter, we find our best friend,
A symphony of giggles that never shall end.

Flora's Song Unfurled

In a meadow where petals take flight,
A daisy cracked jokes, with pure delight.
Laughter erupts, from blossoms quite bold,
Tales of their yarns, that never get old.

Whimsical sounds, as leaves start to sway,
Even the rocks join, in a playful display.
Cacti tell puns, with spines all aglow,
While violets giggle, putting on a show.

Chirps and whispers, nature's own choir,
In this wild theater, hearts lift higher.
Grasshoppers leap, with a comic refrain,
In this floral fiesta, no one's mundane.

Life's twirling dance, it winks and it spins,
With blossoms so clever, where humor begins.
Together they flourish, in a bright array,
A celebration of laughter, day after day.

Vivid Tales of Growth

In a plot where the colors ignite and burst,
Every bloom has a story, for better or worse.
A dandelion grins, so proud of its fluff,
While the orchids just laugh, saying, "We're tough!"

Sunshine and giggles, they sprinkle the ground,
Bringing forth tales, from the whispers around.
A tulip trips lightly, in a jubilant flair,
While the marigolds chuckle, without a care.

Roots are all chattering, beneath the soft clay,
Sharing the splendors of the light of the day.
A wildflower's tale, with humor and cheer,
In this whimsical garden, there's always good beer.

So join in the fun, and let laughter take flight,
In this vibrant place, everything feels right.
With petals and leaves, let the stories entwine,
For in every garden, there's room for divine!

Dance of the Flaming Blossom

In a garden where flowers waltz,
The bright blooms sway without faults.
One flower trips, oh what a sight,
It rolls and giggles, pure delight.

Petals twirl in the warm breeze,
A dance-off that aims to please.
Daisies cheer, while roses pout,
Who knew plants could be about?

Bumblebees buzz with glee around,
As laughter shakes the ground.
Sunshine smiles on this funny scene,
Flaming blossoms live their dream.

With silly moves and pollen spins,
The garden party now begins.
Join the fun, with blooms so bold,
Watch the tales of blooms unfold!

Serenade Under Sunlit Canopies

Beneath the trees, a choir hums,
With leafy hats and drumming thumbs.
Jokes ping-pong between the leaves,
While nature giggles, no reprieves.

The sunlight sneaks, it plays a prank,
On squirrels busy; oh, how they yank!
They lose their acorns in the chase,
As branches sway with a smiling face.

A wobbly fern decides to sing,
About the joys that spring can bring.
Chirping birds join the melody,
What a funny harmony!

Every stem sways, it can't resist,
The joyful tunes they can't dismiss.
So gather 'round this leafy scene,
And share a laugh; let's keep it green!

Vibrant Echoes of Nature

In colors bright, the blossoms shout,
While chubby bumblebees flit about.
A rose trips on its own perfume,
Sending daisies into a fume.

Yellow tulips laugh in the field,
As petals dance; it's a funny shield.
With every breeze, they shake and quake,
Nature's comic, no time to fake.

The violets tell wild tales of glee,
While butterflies sip their sweet tea.
Crimson poppies tumble with flair,
Creating a scene beyond compare.

Shouts of joy resonate near,
From playful plants without a fear.
Together they prance, make no mistake,
In vibrant echoes, the laughter wakes!

A Symphony of Bold Colors

The petals clash like drums in tune,
Blowing bright sirens, afternoon.
With every hue, a tale they weave,
A humorous plot, you won't believe.

Orange and pink hang out to play,
With goofy grins, they steal the day.
A potted plant tries to break dance,
But topples over—what a romance!

The violets snicker, sharing a jest,
While sunflowers wear their crowns with zest.
A dandelion throws in a spin,
And with a giggle, the show begins.

In this bold mix, the laughs unfold,
A colorful symphony, brave and bold.
Join the chorus of nature's song,
As plants remind us where we belong!

Harmonies in Hidden Valleys

In valleys where the flowers play,
Each petal sings the light of day.
The bees do dance, while ants parade,
In floral hats, a grand charade.

With colors bright, they strut and giggle,
The butterflies all dance and wiggle.
A snail in shades of polka dots,
Claims title of the best of spots.

Oh, look at that! A lizard prances,
In rhythm with the sun, it glances.
A chatter of the blooms we'd see,
In joyful tones, a symphony!

So gather round, let laughter rise,
In hidden valleys, hear the cries.
Of nature's fun and frolic days,
Where blooms just live in playful ways.

Portrait of a Blooming Spirit

A flower struts with colors bold,
In potpourri of tales retold.
With every glance, it winks and beams,
A cheeky soul, or so it seems.

In fancy hats of green and pink,
It shares its secrets, won't you think?
Its petals laugh, oh what a sight,
Each bloom a spark of pure delight.

The dew drops dress in sparkly glee,
While critters take a selfie spree.
A joyful buzz fills up the air,
With vibrant life's electric flair.

So here we raise a cup of cheer,
To blooms that sway and spread the cheer.
Their spirit shines in every hue,
In nature's art, a lively view.

Nature's Flamenco

Oh, petals whirl with flair divine,
In gardens where the sun does shine.
Each bloom a dancer, bold and bright,
They twirl and stomp in pure delight.

The bumblebees, they take the lead,
While daisies clap, they plant the seed.
With leaves that rustle, laugh, and sway,
A floral dance, come join the fray!

A ladybug joins in the fun,
Two butterflies dance just as one.
Each pluck of stem, a lively beat,
In nature's ball, they move their feet.

So if you wander, stop and see,
This grand fiesta of nature's glee.
Where petals sing in joyful song,
In nature's flamenco, we belong!

The Language of Brightness

In gardens lush, bright colors talk,
They paint the world, no need to squawk.
With every shade, a tale unfolds,
Of laughter shared and friendships bold.

A sunflower shouts with glee and pride,
While roses giggle, side by side.
Each hue a word, each stem a phrase,
In nature's tongue, we drift and graze.

The petals wink in morning light,
And whisper secrets through the night.
A mellow breeze, a giggling breeze,
With every bud, our hearts they tease.

So let us bloom with tongues of cheer,
In the language bright, from far and near.
Where laughter grows and joy takes flight,
In colors bold, we feel the light.

Rhapsody in Red

In a garden, oh so bright,
A flower with a feathered sight,
It dances in the sun's warm glow,
With leaves that wave, a vibrant show.

A parrot squawks, "Look at me!"
The petals laugh in glee,
They twirl and spin their silky tails,
With whispers of bloom in fragrant trails.

They play with bees, a buzzing crowd,
Who sip from cups, both sweet and loud,
A party under skies of blue,
Where every bud gets a debut!

In evening light, they strike a pose,
A floral fashion week, who knows?
With petals crisp and colors bold,
These jests in bloom are purest gold.

Serenade of the Stalks

On tall, green legs, they sway and bend,
With cheeky smiles, they don't pretend,
Each stem a dancer, proud and spry,
With swirling moves that catch the eye.

A ladybug sings with flair,
As blossoms twirl without a care,
They giggle with a sunbeam's touch,
And wink at bugs that dance too much.

When raindrops land, they shimmy tight,
Embracing all in pure delight,
A wet and wild, splashy spree,
Where splendor joins in jubilee.

Each petal's tip, a flute to play,
They serenade the brightening day,
With rhythms that the wind concurs,
In nature's dance, they sing, they purrs.

Echoes of Elegance

In velvet hues, a cheeky bloom,
With laughter spilling from its room,
It poses with a sassy flair,
In elegant style, beyond compare.

Each petal draped like fancy dress,
They hold a party, who'd guess?
A spritz of dew, a tap of feet,
Laughter rings out, oh what a treat!

With whispers soft, the breezes twine,
As florals gossip, oh so fine,
A banquet set with nectar sweet,
Where every sip's a silly feat.

As shadows lengthen, still they play,
In pursuit of joy till end of day,
These blooms of style, they surely know,
That humor's light makes praises grow.

Flora's Heartbeat

In every petal, a secret hum,
With rhythms from each buzzing drum,
They beat with flair, oh what a cheer,
A floral fiesta held each year!

With jazzy moves, the bees employ,
A buzzing band brings bumble joy,
Each flower taps its vibrant toes,
As laughter lifts and freely flows.

A wind whooshes in for a spin,
With twirls of petals, let the fun begin,
They sway to tunes of sun and air,
With nature's laughter everywhere!

As twilight falls, they pose anew,
A final bow, a bright adieu,
In Flora's heart, the beats resound,
In joyous blooms, pure joy is found.

Stories from the Stem

In the garden, tales unfold,
A flower with a heart of gold.
Whispers of petals, laughter so bright,
Dancing in sun, oh what a sight.

The stem winks with a silly grin,
Telling secrets of where it's been.
A bee buzzes by, can't help but cheer,
'You bloom so fine, you have no fear!'

With raindrops as jewels, they flash and play,
A carnival in bloom, come join the fray!
Leafy jokes float in the gentle breeze,
A plant party happening, oh yes, please!

So gather 'round, you flowers and buds,
Life's too short for gloomy thuds.
Let's shake our colors, let laughter gleam,
In this green kingdom, we're living the dream!

Palette of the Heart

A splash of red, a touch of green,
In every shade, a silly scene.
With rosy blush and leaves of cheer,
This garden smiles from ear to ear.

A paintbrush dipped in morning dew,
Strokes of joy in every hue.
Petals giggle in florescent light,
Creating a rainbow, oh what a sight!

The colors clash, a wild ballet,
As bees and blooms join in the play.
An artist's dream, no room for gloom,
A vibrant party in every room!

So come and paint, no master's touch,
Just let your heart be bold and such.
In this palette, laughter's the art,
Join the revelry, get moving, smart!

Blossoms in Time

Tick tock, hear the petals chime,
A flower's joke is worth a dime.
They bloom and bend, they laugh and sway,
In this moment, we romp and play.

Time slips by with every breeze,
Making memories as sweet as peas.
The tulips tell of years gone past,
While daisies giggle, oh, what a blast!

Each blossom winks with glee and jest,
In this garden, we're truly blessed.
Forget your worries, dance like a bee,
In the laughter of blooms, we're wild and free!

So let's toast to moments, one by one,
With petals of joy, our hearts weigh a ton.
As blossoms march on, in rhythms prime,
We celebrate life with blossoms in time!

Veins of Vitality

In each leaf, a tale untold,
Of sunny days and raindrop gold.
Through veins that pulse with lively cheer,
A plant's own story, crystal clear.

Beneath the surface, wiggles grow,
A party in the roots, oh what a show!
Nutrients dance in vibrant streams,
Filling the leaves with leafy dreams.

Every leaf's a funny face,
In this garden, we find our place.
The roots play games like hide and seek,
In this wild life, who needs to be meek?

So raise a toast to greens so fine,
In veins of joy, let laughter shine.
With every breath, we spin and sway,
In this plant parade, come join the play!

Blooming Beats of the Rainforest

In the jungle, flowers groove,
Dancing leaves, they start to move,
Buzzing bees all sing along,
Nature's beat, a bouncy song.

Loud frogs croak a vibrant tune,
While monkeys swing 'neath the moon,
Petals flutter, colors blend,
Every bloom knows how to trend.

Sassy vines hang on to trees,
Making faces in the breeze,
All the critters join the fest,
In the jungle, life is best!

From the ground up to the sky,
Nothing's shy, oh my, oh my!
With each bloom a laugh appears,
Rolling joy, no room for tears.

In the Arms of Verdant Beauty

Hugging ferns and leafy pals,
Caterpillars throw wild balls,
Rustling fronds join in the cheer,
Winking flowers, never fear!

Chasing shadows, sunlight plays,
Poking fun through leafy maze,
Silly squirrels begin to tease,
Dropping acorns like they're bees.

Unruly vines climb here and there,
Tickling noses everywhere,
Laughter echoes, buzz and hum,
Nature's joy, a tasty crumb!

In this world of green delight,
Giggles dance in morning light,
Every glance, an embrace true,
Verdant arms, we're all askew!

Brushstrokes of Joy

With a swipe of vibrant hue,
Petals burst like morning dew,
Brushstrokes on a canvas bright,
Nature's art, a pure delight.

Daffy dandelions shout,
"Look at me! I'm all about!"
While tulips wear a goofy grin,
Join the fun, let laughter win!

Canvas tapestries unfold,
Whimsical stories yet untold,
A painter's palette comes alive,
In this place where all can thrive.

Every color finds a friend,
Together, joy that won't suspend,
Fluttering wings, playful tease,
In this world, we laugh with ease.

The Lament of a Silent Garden

In a garden, whispers sigh,
Flowers droop, and vines ask why.
Beetles wear their tiny frowns,
As the sun slowly drowns.

"Where's the disco? Where's the light?"
Chirping crickets take to flight,
Hiding under leaves so wide,
Waiting for the fun to bide.

Tired petals droop and pout,
Dreaming of a fun-filled route,
Where the sun becomes a star,
And silliness is never far.

But then a breeze, a gentle wave,
"Fear not, dear blooms, be brave!
Soon the fiesta will commence,
Till then, let's make some nonsense!"

Blooming with Purpose

In a garden where laughter plays,
Flowers wiggle in sunny rays.
Each petal flaunts a silly grin,
Waving hello with vibrant skin.

They whisper jokes that make us laugh,
Sharing secrets on their leafy path.
A bloom skips past, with leaps so fleet,
Saying gardening is quite the treat!

With colors bright, they jest and tease,
Dodging bumblebees with playful ease.
Each bud knows how to steal the show,
In this lively land, all spirits glow.

So come and join this flowery spree,
Where petals dance, wild and free.
With roots in humor, they stand proud,
A joyous garden, laughing loud.

Symphony of Tones

In the garden, a band does play,
With floral notes that sway all day.
A trumpet vine shouts out a tune,
While daisies dance beneath the moon.

The roses croon their lovely song,
As bees buzz in, they hum along.
Sweet violets play a soft refrain,
Stirring up delight in sunny rain.

Orchids twirl in a jazzy beat,
While marigolds stomp their little feet.
Each color joins the raucous fun,
Creating harmony, everyone.

So let us sway with laughter bright,
In this floral concert, pure delight.
With every bloom, a note unfolds,
A whimsical tale that never grows old.

Secrets of the Tropics

In the tropics, where mischief brews,
Palms tell tales that amuse the views.
A frangipani wiggles with glee,
Sharing secrets with a giggling tree.

Banana leaves chuckle and sway,
Whispering stories about their day.
With each twist and turn, they boast their flair,
Ready to share, if you dare to dare!

Cacti sport shades that prick and poke,
Laughing at jokes only plants invoke.
"Why don't we bake?" a hibiscus cries,
"To make some pie with sunshine fries!"

So venture forth, explore the green,
Where laughter flows, and fun is seen.
In every corner of this lush domain,
Tropical secrets unite in refrain.

A Chorus of Color

A chorus bursts in hues so bright,
Colors clash, and it's quite a sight.
Red sings loud, while yellow sings high,
Blue whispers secrets to the sky.

Petunias prance with polka-dot flair,
Dancing in summer's warm, sweet air.
Each hue plays its own vibrant role,
Filling the garden with silly soul.

Lavender laughs, a soothing tune,
While sunflowers spin like a cartoon.
With petals strewn in joyful array,
They frolic and twirl the day away.

So join this party of colors bright,
Where laughter blooms, with pure delight.
A joyful chorus, merry and spry,
In garden stage, let spirits fly!

Petals of Resilience

In a garden, petals shout,
This flower has no doubt.
Staying bright through thick and thin,
Laughing at the wind's din.

Bouncing back with vibrant flair,
Waves a leaf, like it don't care.
With a wink, it bends with ease,
Joking with the swaying breeze.

Colors clash in cheeky art,
A dance that's full of heart.
Wobbling stems in playful guise,
This bloom won't wear a disguise.

Through the rain and all the fuss,
It chuckles on the trampling bus.
A little resilience with each climb,
Making gardening seem sublime.

Harmony in Scarlet

In scarlet robes, it prances bold,
Telling tales that don't get old.
With a grin that shakes the sun,
　Even morning glories run.

Swaying to a funky beat,
　Inviting all the bees to eat.
"Come on, join my flower jam!"
　Starts a party, yes, it can!

Blushing petals catch a breeze,
Tickling each and every leaf.
It's a dance of cherry cheer,
Laughter growing while we're near.

With the sun, it forms a team,
Creating quite a glorious scheme.
In every garden, it's the star,
Chasing clouds away from far.

Heartbeat of the Tropics

In the tropics, life's a race,
This flower's got a happy pace.
Beating bright like a drum so loud,
Dancing 'neath a cheery cloud.

With a pulse of fiery red,
It wakes the sleepy, it's widespread.
Every breeze becomes a laugh,
As roots tickle in the path.

Bouncing blooms in hearty cheer,
Shaking off every single fear.
From the laughter of the sun,
To the games that never run.

It opens up with flair and grace,
Shows the world a laughing face.
In the laughter of the leaves,
The heartbeat of joy believes.

Whispering Leaves

In the shade where whispers bloom,
Leaves conspire to lift the gloom.
Giggling softly in the trees,
"Let's tickle all the buzzing bees!"

Tales of folly, tales of fun,
In the warmth of golden sun.
Frolicing in a leafy maze,
Turning heads in sunny rays.

Every breeze brings gales of glee,
Dancing leaves, quite wild and free.
Twirling round like they just won,
A leaf parade has just begun!

With a chuckle, they take flight,
Playing hide-and-seek with light.
In the green, a funny chat,
Nature's joke, how 'bout that?

Secrets of the Verdant Realm

In a garden where whispers thrive,
Plants converse, oh how they jive!
With leaves that wiggle, stems that dance,
A party starts at every glance.

Frogs in bow ties croak a tune,
While bees buzz in a sweet cartoon.
Flowers wear hats, big and bright,
Each petal has a hidden delight.

Lizards joke in leafy shade,
"I found a shade that won't soon fade!"
Rabbits giggle, tails all a-fluff,
"Oh dear, it seems we've had enough!"

With each sprout, joy fills the air,
Nature's laughter everywhere.
In the realm where green is king,
Life's a riot, let's all sing!

Embrace of the Vibrant Soul

A sunflower winks, what a sight,
Swaying softly, oh, pure delight!
Tulips titter in colors so bold,
Whispering secrets that never grow old.

The roses gossip, petals aflame,
"Did you hear? We're all the same!"
Daisies prance with a playful spin,
They giggle and shout, "Let's begin!"

Cacti boast about their tough skin,
"Poke me!" they cry, with a cheeky grin.
Grass blades stretch, competing for height,
"Who's the tallest?" they ask with delight.

Amidst the laughter, nature's jest,
Blooms and buds are dressed to impress.
In this wild, colorful spree,
Every petal laughs with glee!

Echoes in Petals

In every bloom, a giggle sings,
Nature's humor on vibrant wings.
Petals rustle, sharing a jest,
All the flowers come to rest.

A dandelion, with fluff so round,
Says, "Make a wish, let joy abound!"
The lilies nod, so soft and sweet,
Together, they concoct a treat.

A butterfly flits with vibrant flair,
Telling tales of a breezy affair.
"Is that a flower or a fancy hat?"
The daisies laugh, "Oh, imagine that!"

Their colors sing a comedic rhyme,
In a world where laughter climbs.
Nature's chorus, light and bright,
In petals, echoes of delight!

The Allure of Nature's Palette

In a meadow painted with glee,
Each color shimmers, carefree.
Oranges and pinks in a playful stance,
Nature's canvas, let's all dance!

With splashes of green and hints of gold,
Every petal has a tale to be told.
"Who wore it better?" the blooms debate,
As butterflies flutter, oh, it's fate!

A marigold boasts about her bright hue,
"Follow my lead, I'll show you what's new!"
While the violets grin with a wink,
"Join this party, come take a drink!"

And so, in this vibrant fairyland,
Laughter weaves through every strand.
Nature's palette, a riotous game,
In every bloom, a spark of the same!

The Essence of Flora

In gardens bright, a dance unfolds,
With petals soft, their secrets told.
A flower's grin, a cheeky tease,
Winking slyly in the breeze.

Bumblebees buzz in silly flight,
Chasing dreams from morn to night.
With vibrant hues, they laugh and play,
In nature's game, they lead the way.

Pollen party, join the spree,
Who knew flowers could be so free?
Plants wear hats, and grass wears shoes,
In this bright world, there's none to lose.

And when the rain comes splish and splash,
The flora giggle, a jolly bash.
Each drop a joke, each leaf a grin,
In this wild garden, let joy begin!

Serenity in Bloom

Oh, flowers soft, you wear your charm,
With petals bright, you work your balm.
In sunlit fields, you sway and beam,
A botanical sitcom, the ultimate dream.

The daisies whisper, "Look at me!"
With low-key sass, they're wild and free.
Tulips shimmy in their finest dress,
While dandelions make a big mess.

Harmonies of color in a striking show,
They gossip lightly, with a summer glow.
With every breeze, they share a tale,
Of pollen parties on a sail.

In the quiet mischief of afternoon sun,
Floral hilarity has just begun.
Nature's laughter in fragrant array,
A whimsical ballet that never will fray!

Floral Echoes of Love

A rose declares, "I'm quite the catch!"
"It's not just a bloom, it's a perfect match!"
The violets giggle, a crush in bloom,
As bumblebees plot their next big zoom.

Lavender sighs, "I'm scented perfection,"
Reminding us all of love's sweet affection.
Forget-me-nots wink with a cute little nod,
Spreading cheer in the garden of God.

Orchids strut in a glamorous way,
Turning heads on a sunny day.
In floral comedy, love takes flight,
With every petal, a heart ignites!

While daisies declare, "We're friends, not foes!"
In this silly patch, affection grows.
Through giggles and blooms, let's cheer and sway,
For love in the garden is here to stay!

Vivacity of Variegation

In vibrant hues and patterns grand,
Flowers show life, hand in hand.
With every glance, a grin does spark,
Their colors dance from light till dark.

Marigolds boast in lively attire,
While sunflowers reach for dreams higher.
With all their quirks, they start a trend,
Nature's show-offs, round every bend.

Petunias chime in with vibrant tunes,
As garden parties commence in June.
"Let's celebrate our wild design!"
A floral fiesta, oh, how divine!

From violets to poppies, all join the fun,
A kaleidoscope riot, bright in the sun.
With laughter and color, each bloom has its fate,
In vivacious life, they dance and create!

Radiant Journeys

In a pot, with sunshine bright,
Dancing leaves show off delight.
Vibrant blooms wear smiles wide,
Tickling bees on a joyful ride.

Funny hats on plants so grand,
Making sure they make a stand.
With a wink and a playful cheer,
They sway like they just don't care here.

In gardens where the mischief grows,
Each petal tells wild, silly prose.
A parade of colors, bright and bold,
In this plant world, stories unfold.

So when you see that bouncy sprout,
Remember its giggles; that's no doubt.
With roots in laughter, a joyful spree,
This plant sure knows how fun life can be!

Whispers of the Untamed

Beneath the moon, where wild winds play,
A riot of colors leads the way.
Petals that chuckle, leaves that prance,
In this garden, life's a dance!

Lively laughter among the greens,
Swaying gently, what a scene!
Crickets join in, creating sound,
While the flowers spin round and round.

And when the sun begins to rise,
They're still giggling, oh what a surprise!
With dewdrops glistening on a whim,
Each petal's humor never dim.

Nature's jesters, always in bloom,
Filling the air with joy and zoom.
So dance along with blooms so bright,
Let them whisper the world, alright!

Tints of Tranquility

In peaceful shades, a flower hums,
With giggles hidden in quiet thums.
Soft as down, but bold in cheer,
Their whispers tickle those who near.

Gentle greens and purples blend,
While petals giggle, they won't end.
A secret world where calm meets fun,
Underneath the golden sun.

Tea parties hosted for bugs and bees,
Relaxing under the leafy trees.
A clumsy butterfly trips and falls,
While flowers crack up in wild calls.

Oh what a serene scene it makes,
With laughter stirring like gentle wakes.
So join the fun, in tranquil light,
Where humor blooms in the quiet night!

Floral Legacies

In history's garden, tales unfold,
Where flowers chuckle, bold and gold.
Petals reminiscent of days gone by,
Swaying in rhythm, oh so spry!

Ancient blooms with stories grand,
Leave their messages throughout the land.
A giggle here, a wink there,
Their legacy lives with casual flair.

Chasing shadows of shadows past,
These quirky plants are built to last.
Each playful petal knows its part,
Making sure to capture hearts.

Floral jokes passed down the line,
Wit and whimsy intertwine.
So when you stroll through nature's show,
Remember the laughs that flowers know!

Elegance in a Crimson Kiss

In the garden, I'm so bright,
I stand out, a real delight.
With leaves like fans, I wave with glee,
Watch the bees come dance with me!

My petals shine in sultry glow,
I laugh at weeds, so tall and slow.
The sun winks down, says, "Give a show!"
While frogs croak out a goofy hello!

Tapestry of Tropical Dreams

In a jungle filled with charm,
I strut along, causing alarm.
The parrots squawk, they think I'm fab,
I strike a pose, it's quite the blab!

Bouncing tunes with every sway,
I steal the spotlight, come what may.
With vibrant hues, I paint the scene,
A plant diva, living the dream!

Ritual of the Radiant Flower

Every morning, I preen and pose,
With a giggle, as sunlight flows.
The world does pause, to hear my flair,
As butterflies join, up in the air!

I've got style, I've got grace,
Every bloom's in a funny race.
With roots so bold and leaves that tease,
I giggle with the fluttering breeze!

The Melody of Flora's Heart

In a patch of earth, I sing a tune,
With every bloom, I bust a move.
The critters clap, they know the rhyme,
As bees buzz in, it's party time!

Swing with me, oh foliage friends,
Our laughter dances, never ends.
With colors bold, our joy's a spark,
The garden giggles, light and dark!

Amour in Bloom

In a garden of hearts, love doth conspire,
With petals of pink that never tire.
They whisper sweet nothings to the breeze,
Inviting the bees to join in with ease.

A butterfly swoops with a wink and a twirl,
Each flower a giggle, each stem a swirl.
They dance in the aroma of love's fine perfume,
Promising laughter to forever bloom.

Dances in the Sunlight

When sunlight cascades on a merry parade,
Each leaf in the breeze feels happily swayed.
The petals take flight in a comical spin,
As insects join in on the joyful din.

A ladybug twirls in a red polka dot,
While caterpillars join for a dance, believe it or not!
The flowers all giggle, under sun's bright gaze,
Crafting a party that lasts all day.

Petal Dreams and Shadows

In the soft light of dusk, dreams take their flight,
Where petals tell secrets, both quirky and light.
The shadows do flutter, with whispers so sly,
As frustrated bugs raise a puzzled sigh.

A jovial snail makes his slow debut,
On a leaf full of dreams, and more than a few.
They laugh at the sky, so endless and grand,
Blooming in mischief, all perfectly planned.

Caress of a Summer Breeze

A summer breeze tickles the flowers so round,
They sway and they giggle at the joys that abound.
With petals like laughter, they sway side to side,
As butterflies hesitate, too shy to glide.

The daisies start teasing, "We're brighter, you see!"
While sunflowers strut in their tall jubilee.
They bask in the warmth, with a silly twist,
Creating a joy that can't be missed!

Tales from a Blooming Heart

In the garden, a party unfolds,
Plants wear tuxedos, so bold!
Petals dance to the sun's delight,
Leaves gossip late into the night.

Bees buzz in for a snack, oh dear,
Slipping on pollen, they cheer!
A cactus jokes, sharp wit in bloom,
While sunflowers sway to the boom!

A rogue fern flirts with a shy vine,
"Come on, let's twist, it'll be fine!"
Marigolds chuckle, their scent's so sweet,
A wild party, with nature's heartbeat!

So gather round, all green and bright,
Join the laughter, a pure delight!
In this patch of joy, love's art,
We sing together from the heart!

Echoing Vibrations of Nature

A serenade of colors bright,
Flora invites all to the night.
"Did you hear the blooms take a stand?"
They jest with vines, a lively band!

The daisies laugh, "We've got style!"
Tulips blush, they can't help but smile.
Petals tickle with a gentle tease,
"Spring's our season, do as we please!"

Swaying with rhythm, a breeze comes by,
Buds are winking, oh my, oh my!
Tree branches nod, keeping the beat,
While roots tap-dance beneath our feet!

So join us here, where laughter flows,
In a garden where anything goes!
Echoing joy, a natural tune,
Under the watchful eye of the moon!

Reflections in Red

In a splash of red, the fun begins,
Blushing petals, wearing grins.
"Let's play tag!" cries a cheeky rose,
While daisies bloom, striking a pose.

The sun shines bright, a swirling light,
A playful breeze gives blooms a fright!
"Hold still!" laughs a sly, emerald leaf,
As the petals wiggle in disbelief!

Buzzing bees bring their silly buzz,
"Here comes trouble!" the tulips fuzz.
"Who's the fairest of us all?"
A sunflower giggles, "Just watch me stand tall!"

So here we dance, each petal a hiccup,
With laughter ripe inside this cup.
Reflections sparkling, bright and fed,
In this garden, wear your red!

The Spirit of the Greenhouse

Inside the house where green things grow,
Plants converse, their spirits flow.
"I'm taller now," a young sprout squeaks,
While herbs exchange their fragrant tweaks.

Chlorophyll raves, "This breeze feels nice!"
Overhead, a bulb makes a surprise slice.
"Who ordered this spotlight?" it inquires,
While hanging plants sway like rock stars' choirs.

A pot of mint tries to break the ice,
"Join my dance, it'll be so nice!"
Tomatoes chuckle, red and plump,
In this wild greenhouse, we laugh, we jump!

So gather friends, your roots so dear,
Let's bloom together, have no fear!
With every leaf, a joy to share,
In this spirit, life's beyond compare!

A Canvas of Life

In a garden where colors clash,
Petals wear a bright mustache,
Dancing plants in a silly show,
Wiggling leaves say hello, no?

Fruits and blooms in a wild air,
A monkey swings without a care,
Laughing buds with jokes to share,
Nature's laugh – beyond compare!

Bumblebees, with buzzy cheer,
Enroll in class, no need to fear,
Their dance is quirky, what a sight,
Pollinate and take flight at night!

So let us join this merry scene,
With flowers dressed in vibrant green,
A canvas painted with pure glee,
Life's fun with plants, can't you see?

Flourish Beneath a Tropical Sky

Underneath a sun so bright,
Leaves throw parties, what a sight!
Swinging lianas, having fun,
Hula-hooping 'round the sun!

Coconuts in a champion race,
Rolling swiftly, keeping pace,
Palm trees giggle with delight,
As seagulls argue - who takes flight?

Colorful blooms with silly grins,
Gossiping about the winds' spins,
A dance of petals in the breeze,
Nature laughs, it's sure to please!

Whispers of joy from roots below,
Sharing secrets, don't you know?
Flourish here, beneath the beams,
Life's a joke stitched from our dreams!

Ode to the Exotic Bloom

Oh exotic bloom, with flair so grand,
A top-notch dancer in the land,
You twirl and sway, what a show,
Sprouting laughter wherever you grow!

Your colors burst like morning light,
Mimicking a clown in pure delight,
The bees can't help but join the spree,
As you flaunt your charm so breezy!

A chatty flower with tales to spin,
Of raindrops dancing and cheeky wind,
You wink and nod, so full of cheer,
An invitation to laugh and leer!

Oh bloom, you brighten every street,
Sprigs of joy, our lives replete,
In your lush realm, we all find glee,
An ode to laughs - just let it be!

Caress of the Morning Dew

Morning dew, a soft embrace,
Kissing blooms, a playful race,
Plants giggle, shake off the night,
With droplets sparkling, oh what a sight!

Sunrise breaks with vibrant hues,
Dewy friends sip on their brews,
Leafy eyebrows raised in fun,
"Another day, let's run, run, run!"

Clouds peek in with a cheeky grin,
"Did you hear the one about a fin?"
Flowers stop to chuckle in style,
Each petal grinning with a smile!

So take a stroll at break of day,
Where laughter blooms and flowers play,
The caress of dew so light and spry,
Reminds us all to give joy a try!

Luminescence of Life

In the garden where colors clash,
Petals shine like a neon splash,
Bees wear sunglasses, quite a sight,
Dancing and buzzing, oh what a delight!

Frogs play hopscotch on vibrant leaves,
While butterflies plot their sunny heaves,
The sun makes a joke, it's quite absurd,
And flowers giggle, not saying a word.

In this blossom of whims and cheer,
Every day feels like New Year's here,
A jasmine jester jokes with a rose,
As laughter twirls with the gentle blows.

So let's all clap for the bloom's best show,
With petals winking from head to toe,
Nature's comedy, a laugh we can share,
In this floral circus, we have flair!

Blush of a Petal

A petal blushed, oh what a tease,
Winking at the bumblebees,
It prances under the hazy sun,
Saying, 'Come join the floral fun!'

A daisy told a joke to a sprout,
But the tulip just couldn't figure it out,
Weeds rolled their eyes, they are such clowns,
While roses wear their thorny crowns.

The sun dips low with a playful grin,
And shadows dance, let the fun begin,
A flutter of petals, they twirl and sway,
In this garden, laughter leads the way!

So come and sip the nectar's brew,
As petals gossip, 'Did you hear the news?'
In this realm of colors and whimsy bright,
Each bloom's a character, what a sight!

Symbol of the Sublime

In fields where whimsy starts to bloom,
A flower wiggles, making room,
With petals shaped like a crooked smile,
It beckons us, let's stay awhile!

Leaves are laughing, the grass is wild,
Even the cactus looks like a child,
Every blossom's a tiny sage,
With stories told on an endless page.

In gardens of giggles and sunny rays,
Where even the thorns have quirky ways,
Nature's laughter fills the airy space,
Join in the fun, let's pick up the pace!

So here's to blooms and their laughter spree,
In this floral world, you must agree,
Each petal whispers a joke so fine,
A symbol of joy, pure and divine!

Euphony of Botanicals

In a chorus where petals sing,
Laughter and sunshine take to wing,
A rose cracked a joke at a pansy's expense,
While bees buzzed in with their buzzing wit hence.

The lilacs chuckled, and daisies chimed,
Nature's own band, rhythmically rhymed,
As the tulips fired off jokes with glee,
The sweet scent of humor wafted free.

While owls hooted in night's embrace,
Violets twinkled in this merry place,
Every leaf whispered tales of the day,
In this botanical play, come what may!

So dance with the daisies, sway with the breeze,
In the laughter of flowers, let worries freeze,
Join this euphony, let your heart thrill,
In the joyful blooms, let's laugh at will!

Petal Poetry

In a garden so bright, flowers bloom with glee,
They whisper sweet secrets, oh can you hear me?
A tulip's bold shout, a daisy's soft giggle,
They dance in the breeze, and make the bees wiggle.

A rose tells a joke, all thorny and sly,
While sunflowers chuckle, reaching for the sky.
Each petal a laugh, in nature's grand play,
Come join the confusion, let's frolic all day!

With a cactus in shades, it pokes a quick pun,
While violets gossip, oh isn't it fun?
Each bud has a tale, a whimsical rhyme,
In this floral fiesta, there's always more time.

So grab your green thumbs, let's plant some delight,
In this silly garden, everything's bright.
With petals for pages, we'll write our own song,
In the book of the blossoms, where we all belong.

Nature's Love Letter

Oh, nature writes letters with ink made of dew,
In crumpled-up pages, with a smile just for you.
Grass blades pen verses, while leaves softly sway,
Caressing the world in the quirkiest way.

The clouds scribble jokes, as they drift in the blue,
Sending puffy whispers on a breeze that feels new.
With each raindrop's tap, it's a rhythmic love beat,
Nature's sweet serenade, oh how it feels sweet!

A squirrel quotes wisdom from the tree's lovely bark,
While flowers join in, adding flair to the spark.
With petals as confetti, they throw such a bash,
In this love letter's rhythm, life giggles with dash.

So read between lines, in the shadows and sun,
Nature's quite silly, when all's said and done.
With laughter in blooms, and humor so bright,
Let's cherish these letters, and savor the light.

The Dance of the Colors

In gardens alive, hues twirl and they spin,
With reds that are cheeky, and yellows that grin.
A violet winks shyly, while oranges burst forth,
In this rainbow parade, joy dances with mirth.

Each blossom's a dancer, with moves oh so sly,
Beneath the warm sun, they leap and they fly.
A tulip does cha-cha while the lilies croon,
All under the light of the big, smiling moon.

Petals frolic freely, while foliage claps hands,
With butterflies swirling like confetti on strands.
The colors sing loudly, a jubilant throng,
In the garden of humor, we all sing along.

So dance with the hues, let your spirit take flight,
In this world of bright laughter, everything's right.
With joy dripping colors, let's paint with our hearts,
In this whimsical waltz, let the fun never part.

Tributes to the Earth

Oh Earth, you're a canvas, painted with flair,
With rivers of laughter and mountains that care.
Your soil holds secrets, all funky and strange,
In this quirky tribute, let's celebrate change.

Waters giggle softly, tickling the shore,
While trees do high-fives, forever wanting more.
Each rock holds a riddle, each sunset a jest,
Nature's grand comedy, we're truly blessed.

The flowers step forward, wearing hats made of fun,
With dandelion wishes under the sun.
They sing tributes loudly, their petals on swell,
In this earth-friendly laughter, all's merry and well.

So let's raise a toast, with a grin and a cheer,
To the quirks of our planet, so charmingly clear.
For in this wild tapestry, where giggles abound,
Nature's our playground, our joy knows no bound.

Beauty's Bright Embrace

In a garden of giggles, petals play,
With colors that dance and sway all day.
A bloom with a wink, it calls to the bees,
"Come sip my sweet nectar, if you please!"

A leaf in a hat, how silly it seems,
Dressing for sunlight, fulfilling its dreams.
With roots that can tickle the ground while it grows,
This flora is full of delightful shows!

The sun plays peek-a-boo, oh what a tease,
While shadows skip past, as happy as breeze.
Crickets take center stage, ready to sing,
To the beat of the blossoms—what joy they bring!

So come take a stroll where the laughter's loud,
Among vibrant blossoms, stand tall and proud.
In this garden of whimsy, let spirits ignite,
With every bright laugh, our joy takes flight!

Lullabies of the Land

As shadows stretch long in the fading light,
The flowers hum softly, such a sweet sight.
Their lullabies twinkle, like stars in the night,
While frogs croak along, what a funny fright!

Each petal a pillow, so cushy and round,
Bouncing along as they dance on the ground.
The wind starts to giggle, swirling in play,
Whispering secrets to end of the day.

A bumblebee chimes in with a buzz,
Adding to melodies, just because.
In this jolly concert, all senses do blend,
Thus nature's own laughter, it never will end.

So if you're feeling tired, just take a rest,
Let this charming symphony be your best quest.
For in every sound, there is joy we can find,
In these lullabies shared by the flowers, so kind!

Blooms of the Unseen

In a world where secrets are hidden in greens,
Lurk blooms full of laughter, none heard, only seen.
With petals that giggle and stalks that can sway,
They whisper of mischief in a sprightly way.

A flower in pjs, so snug and so bright,
Telling its stories beneath the moonlight.
The roots murmur tales, down deep in the earth,
About long-lost blooms and their capricious mirth.

Frogs are the audience, clapping their hands,
As petals stand tall, striking whimsical stands.
With every soft rustle, a chuckle set free,
In this hidden garden, joy's glee is key.

So peek through the leaves, let your laughter soar,
There's magic and mischief behind every door.
For the blooms of the unseen bring smiles so great,
In their jubilant world, come dance with fate!

Shades of Splendor

In the garden of giggles, colors collide,
With shades of splendor, nothing to hide.
The yellow is zany, the pink's in a whirl,
While purple spins circles, what a fun twirl!

A blue lily joked with a cheeky pink rose,
Said, "Let's paint the town!" as they struck a pose.
With reds that can dance, and whites that can leap,
Nature's own comedy, so joyful, no sleep!

The daisies are chuckling, with faces so bright,
Showing off their charms, just for delight.
While sunflowers giggle at clouds passing by,
Their golden crowns shining, reaching up high.

So if you feel grumpy or lost in your day,
Just visit the blooms, let their laughter play.
In the shades of splendor, joy's colors entwine,
For each petal's a punchline, sweet as fine wine!

Virtuosos of the Vines

In the greenest glade, they twirl and sway,
Plants wear tutus, oh what a display!
The vines all giggle as they dance about,
While the flowers whisper, "What's this fuss about?"

Cacti are strumming with no care at all,
While daisies bob up, making a ball!
The sun's a spotlight, it's quite a sight,
In this leafy circus, everything feels right!

Lilies are giggling, so lively and bright,
As twining tendrils dance into the night.
The ivy's a jester, twirling with glee,
It's the botanical fun fair, come join me!

Mossy acrobats leap with no fear,
Daffodils chuckle, raising a cheer.
With potting soil pies and nectar drinks,
Life's a riot here, or so one thinks!

Love's Arboretum

Roses are sipping on sweet lemonade,
While daisies debate their latest parade.
Tulips are tweeting about last night's show,
In this leafy retreat, there's plenty to flow!

Laughter blooms bright in each twist and turn,
As ferns do a jig, oh how they yearn!
The wild vines whisper sweet jokes in the breeze,
Creating a chorus that's sure to please.

Romance is tender in this garden alive,
Bumblebees buzz while butterflies thrive.
A love song plays amongst roots and stems,
Even grumpy herbs can't resist the gems!

Couples of geraniums sway to the beat,
As trunks tap their toes, oh what a treat!
In this arboreal love, there's no need to pout,
With petals aflutter, we dance it all out!

Botanicals in Ballad

Daffodils croon in their sunlit home,
Roses write letters, no need to roam.
Violets are quizzical, pondering fate,
While broccolis bask in a garden state.

Sunflowers break into a cheerful jig,
Composting dreams, both big and gig.
The herbs are harmonizing, a savory tune,
Mixing love potions beneath the bright moon.

Lilacs recite, with a flourish and flair,
Tales of their travels, a botanical dare!
In this green realm, with chuckles and sighs,
Life is a song, and joy never dies.

Chrysanthemums spill secrets so sly,
As potted plants gossip, oh me, oh my!
With roots intertwined, and laughter for days,
Botanicals unite in whimsical ways!

Tranquil Garden Musings

In the silence of petals, thoughts spill like tea,
Bees buzzing gently, as happy as can be.
A snail plays the lute, serenading a leaf,
While daisies exchange their beliefs with relief.

Sweet fragrances waft in a slow, swirling dance,
As the garden keeps spinning in a sunlit trance.
Each branch has a story, each blossom a laugh,
Nature's a poet, writing her own half.

Clouds drift by softly, like whispers of grace,
While shadows below join in this leafy race.
With playful banter in rustling leaves,
A humor-filled tapestry that nature weaves.

The lavender chuckles in violet delight,
Sending giggles floating into the night.
In this tranquil realm, where laughter does bloom,
The garden's alive, in full, fragrant plume!

Heart's Desire in Bloom

A flower in a pot, how grand it grows,
With petals so bright, like a circus show.
It sways in the breeze, a dance of delight,
Wishing for sunlight, just a tad too bright.

The neighbors all gossip, 'What's that in there?'
A vibrant red creature, without a care.
It struts like a peacock, in the garden it plays,
Stealing the show, in unique, funny ways.

A sip of fresh water, a sip of fine tea,
Each leaf gets a laugh, as it waves with glee.
Roots twist and twirl, in a silky ballet,
Making all plants wish they could join the fray.

Heart's desire, it blooms, keeping spirits high,
With a wink and a nudge, it bids the birds fly.
This flower's a joker, a bright little tease,
Bringing smiles to all, with petal-swigging ease.

Petals of Resilience

Oh, the petals stand tall, in spite of the rain,
They giggle at storms, their laughter's insane.
With a splash here and there, they puddle and play,
Still shining like stars at the end of the day.

A dance with the bees, what a sight to behold,
They tickle and tumble, actions so bold.
Petals that shimmer, in colors quite spry,
Look just like clowns, as they wave and comply.

Through weeds and through grass, they spread all their cheer,
Telling each passerby, "Don't shed any tears!"
A tale of resilience, they giggle and say,
"Even when tossed, we'll just sway and display."

Little flowers unite, in great clusters of fun,
Their antics erupt, as they bask in the sun.
With a wink and a chuckle, they bask and they beam,
Petals of resilience, they're living a dream!

A Dance of Vibrant Shades

A dance on the breeze, all colors collide,
Yellow, pink, and crimson, they leap with pride.
Shake off your worries, and join the parade,
These petals for laughter, an art form well-made.

Like clowns in the garden, all silly and spry,
They wiggle and giggle, as butterflies fly.
Spinning around, they won't take a rest,
In their chaotic dance, they're at their best.

Their partners in bloom, those leaves wave in tune,
Creating a symphony beneath the bright moon.
With nature's own music, laughter fills the air,
A joyful assembly, without a single care.

So join in the fun, hear the petals' loud cheer,
In this lively ballet, there's nothing to fear.
For all are invited, just open the door,
To a dance of vibrant shades, and you'll want more!

The Language of Leaves

Oh, listen closely, the leaves have a tale,
They whisper and chuckle, almost like rail.
A rustle of gossip, in sweet, breezy tones,
Talk of the garden, shared from the thrones.

With each gentle sway, they wave to their pals,
Sienne from the daisies, and Vincent from galls.
"Did you hear the news?" says a brave little sprout,
"Bobblo the cactus is dancing about!"

In the shade of the trees, the air fills with laughs,
As comical creatures draw mischievous drafts.
"Let's play a trick on that pompous old rose,"
Their laughter erupts, and the fun only grows.

Through seasons they chatter, with humor so keen,
The language of leaves is the best ever seen.
Join in their union, oh come take a seat,
In the comedy garden, where fibers compete!

www.ingramcontent.com/pod-product-compliance
Lightning Source LLC
Chambersburg PA
CBHW070314120526
44590CB00017B/2680